DRAWING DINOSAURS

DRAWING
GIGANOTOSAURUS
AND OTHER GIANT DINOSAURS

STEVE BEAUMONT

PowerKiDS
press.

New York

Published in 2010 by The Rosen Publishing Group, Inc.
29 East 21st Street, New York, NY 10010

Copyright © 2010 Arcturus Publishing Ltd

Artwork and text: Steve Beaumont
Editor (Arcturus): Carron Brown
Designer: Steve Flight

Library of Congress Cataloging-in-Publication Data

Beaumont, Steve.
  Drawing Giganotosaurus and other giant dinosaurs / Steve Beaumont. — 1st ed.
      p. cm. — (Drawing dinosaurs)
  Includes index.
  ISBN 978-1-61531-905-3 (library binding) — ISBN 978-1-4488-0430-6 (pbk.) —
ISBN 978-1-4488-0431-3 (6-pack)
  1. Dinosaurs in art—Juvenile literature. 2. Drawing—Technique—Juvenile literature.
3. Giganotosaurus—Juvenile literature. I. Title.
  NC780.5.B392 2010
  743.6—dc22
                                    2009033269

Printed in China

CPSIA compliance information: Batch #AW0102PK : For further information contact Rosen Publishing, New York, New York at 1-800-237-9932

CONTENTS

"Dinosaurs"… the word conjures up all kinds of powerful and exciting images. From the massive size of fierce Giganotosaurus to the ground-shaking weight of plant-eating Argentinosaurus and the huge sail-like structure on the back of Spinosaurus—dinosaurs came in all shapes and sizes.

These amazing creatures ruled Earth for over 160 million years until, suddenly, they all died out. No one has ever seen a living, moving, roaring dinosaur, but thanks to the research of paleontologists, who piece together dinosaur fossils, we now have a pretty good idea what many of them looked like.

Some were as big as huge buildings, others had enormous teeth, scaly skin, horns, claws, and body armor. Dinosaurs have played starring roles in books, on television, and in blockbuster movies, and now it's time for them to take center stage on your drawing pad!

In this book we've chosen three incredible meat-eating dinosaurs for you to learn how to draw. We've also included a dinosaur landscape for you to sketch, so you can really set the prehistoric scene for your drawings.

You'll find advice on the essential drawing tools you'll need to get started, tips on how to get the best results from your drawings, and easy-to-follow step-by-step instructions showing you how to draw each dinosaur. So, it's time to bring these extinct monsters back to life—let's draw some dinosaurs!

DRAWING TOOLS

Let's start with the essential drawing tools you'll need to create awesome illustrations. Build up your collection as your drawing skills improve.

LAYOUT PAPER

Artists, both as professionals and as students, rarely produce their first practice sketches on their best quality art paper. It's a good idea to buy some inexpensive plain letter-size paper from a stationery store for all of your practice sketches. Buy the least expensive kind.

Most professional illustrators use cheaper paper for basic layouts and practice sketches before they get to the more serious task of producing a masterpiece on more costly material.

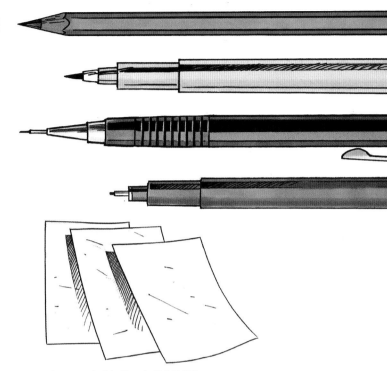

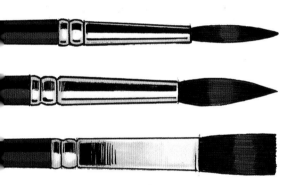

HEAVY DRAWING PAPER

This paper is ideal for your final version. You don't have to buy the most expensive brand—most decent arts and crafts stores will stock their own brand or another lower-priced brand and unless you're thinking of turning professional, these will work fine.

WATERCOLOR PAPER

This paper is made from 100 percent cotton and is much higher quality than wood-based papers. Most arts and crafts stores will stock a large range of weights and sizes—140 pounds per ream (300 g/sq m) will be fine.

LINE ART PAPER

If you want to practice black and white ink drawing, line art paper enables you to produce a nice clear crisp line. You'll get better results than you would on heavier paper as it has a much smoother surface.

PENCILS

It's best not to cut corners on quality here. Get a good range of graphite (lead) pencils ranging from soft (#1) to hard (#4).

Hard lead lasts longer and leaves less graphite on the paper. Soft lead leaves more lead on the paper and wears down more quickly. Every artist has his personal preference, but #2.5 pencils are a good medium grade to start out with until you find your own favorite.

Spend some time drawing with each grade of pencil and get used to their different qualities. Another good product to try is the clutch, or mechanical pencil. These are available in a range of lead thicknesses, 0.5mm being a good medium size. These pencils are very good for fine detail work.

PENS

There is a large range of good quality pens on the market and all will do a decent job of inking. It's important to experiment with a range of different pens to determine which you find most comfortable to work with.

You may find that you end up using a combination of pens to produce your finished piece of artwork. Remember to use a pen that has waterproof ink if you want to color your illustration with a watercolor or ink wash.

It's a good idea to use one of these—there's nothing worse than having your nicely inked drawing ruined by an accidental drop of water!

BRUSHES

Some artists like to use a fine brush for inking linework. This takes a bit more practice and patience to master, but the results can be very satisfying. If you want to try your hand at brushwork, you will definitely need to get some good-quality sable brushes.

ERASER

There are three main types of erasers: rubber, plastic, and putty. Try all three to see which kind you prefer.

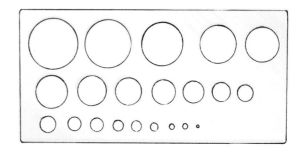

PANTONE MARKERS

These are very versatile pens and with practice can give pleasing results.

INKS

With the rise of computers and digital illustration, materials such as inks have become a bit obscure, so you may have to look harder for these, but most good arts and crafts stores should stock them.

WATERCOLORS AND GOUACHE

Most art stores will stock a wide range of these products, from professional to student quality.

CIRCLE TEMPLATE

This is very useful for drawing small circles.

FRENCH CURVES

These are available in a few shapes and sizes and are useful for drawing curves.

BUILDING DINOSAURS

Notice how a simple oval shape forms the body of these three dinosaurs (figs.1, 2, and 3). Even though they are all very differently shaped, an oval forms the body of each one perfectly.

Fig. 4 shows how a dinosaur can be constructed using all these basic shapes. Cylinders are used for its legs and arms, an oval shape forms its body, and a smaller egg shape is used for its head.

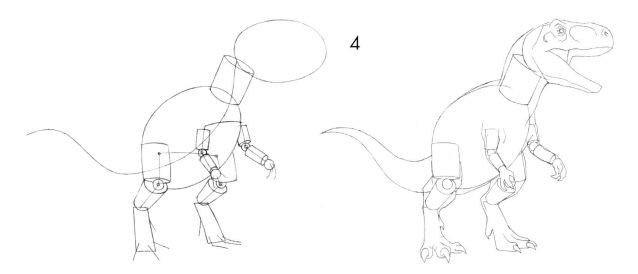

INKING

Once you have completed your dinosaur in pencil, it's time to start inking over the lines for a really dramatic effect. Although you could faithfully follow the pencil drawing, try to vary the thickness of your ink lines for a more interesting and powerful result. Try practicing with different pens and inks.

STEP 1
Here we have a pencil drawing of T. rex.

STEP 2
Follow the pencil line and start inking. Using thicker lines for the folds of skin, wrinkles, and crevices will add depth.

STEP 3
Now apply solid black around the eye and inside the mouth.

STEP 4
By adding some simple hatching around the eye area, it creates extra interest. Attention to detail like this will make your dinosaur look even more realistic.

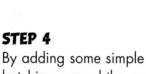

GIGANOTOSAURUS

DINO FACT FILE

Giganotosaurus was discovered in Argentina in 1994 and it's believed to be the largest carnivore due to its overall size—even bigger than T. rex. This terrifying predator measured 45 feet (14 m) in length. Its skull alone was 6 feet (1.8 m) long and housed rows of sharp serrated teeth, each measuring 8 inches (20 cm) in length. Even more scarily, they hunted in packs.

STEP 1
Start with the basic stick figure.

STEP 2
Build its frame using basic construction shapes. Draw a row of short cylinders to create the neck and tail.

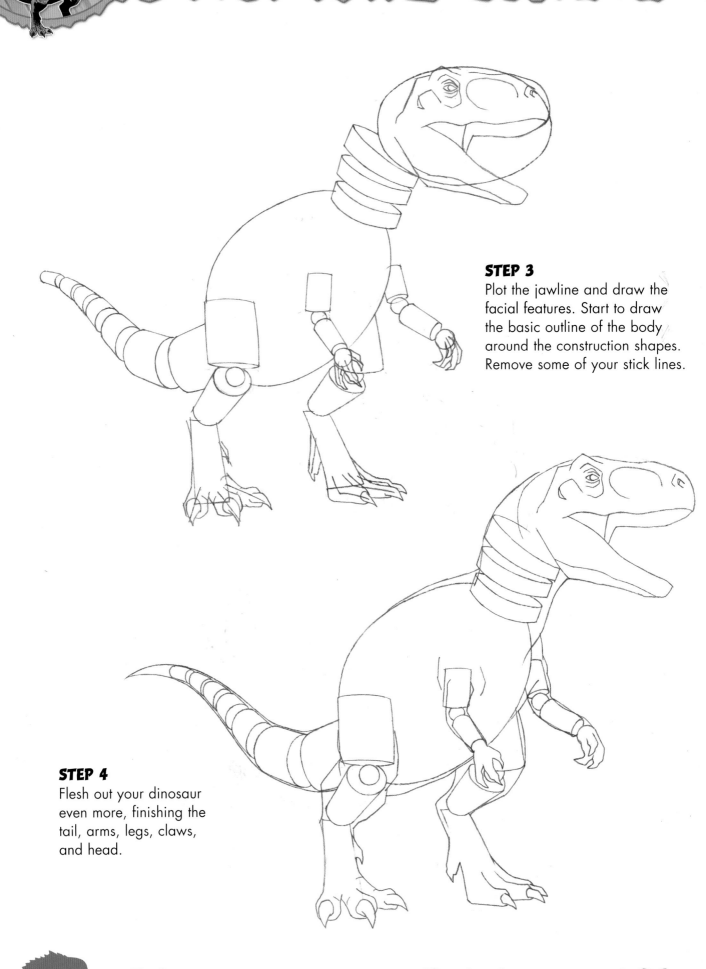

STEP 3

Plot the jawline and draw the facial features. Start to draw the basic outline of the body around the construction shapes. Remove some of your stick lines.

STEP 4

Flesh out your dinosaur even more, finishing the tail, arms, legs, claws, and head.

STEP 5

Now it's time to remove your interior construction shapes. Next draw the teeth and tongue, and start adding detail to the skin. Giganotosaurus had bony spines running down its back and on the top of its head. Leave the areas you want to shade blank.

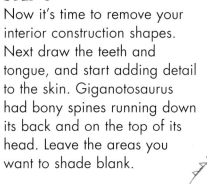

STEP 6

Now finish the final pencil drawing by adding some more detailed scales and all your shading.

DID YOU KNOW?

GIGANOTOSAURUS WAS A GIANT PREDATOR, BUT NOT A VERY SMART ONE. ITS TINY BRAIN WAS THE SIZE AND SHAPE OF A BANANA.

STEP 7

Now ink over the pencil work. Varying the strength of your ink lines will add depth and interest to your final drawing.

STEP 8

Start coloring your Giganotosaurus by applying a sand-colored base all over. Over the top, apply a rusty orange to its back, head, and tail. Add some extra texture and shading to the skin using touches of midrange gray.

SPINOSAURUS

DINO FACT FILE

Spinosaurus, or "spine lizard," was a ferocious meat eater with a massive sail-like structure on its back. Scientists aren't sure what it was for but think it regulated its body temperature. It was the longest carnivore and measured up to 60 feet (18 m) tall—that's bigger than three giraffes stacked on top of each other! They were highly intelligent, with crocodile-like jaws and sharp teeth.

STEP 1
Start by drawing the basic stick figure.

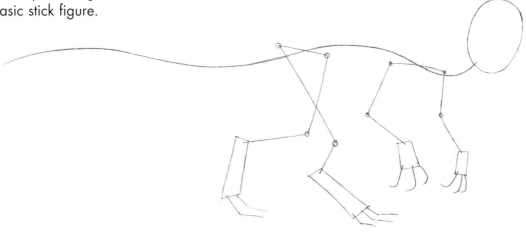

STEP 2
Add your construction shapes. Spinosaurus's jaws are wide open. Draw its face using a triangle for the jaw and a trapezoid for the top of its head.

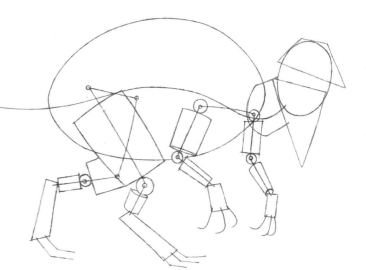

STEP 3

Add the skin by drawing around the shapes. Add a sweeping curve going from the tail to the neck for the dinosaur's big spine. Start to draw in the face and teeth and add the claws.

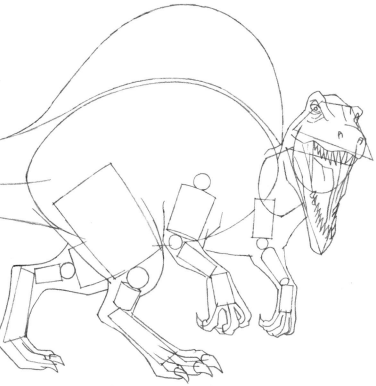

STEP 4

Remove all of your construction shapes and stick lines so you are left with a clean drawing. Add details to the sail-like fin, and to the skin, indicating where shadow will fall.

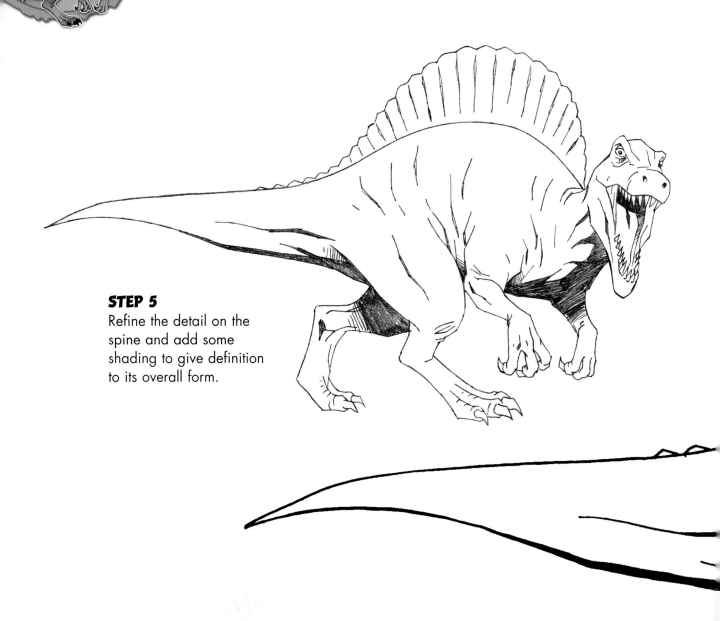

STEP 5
Refine the detail on the spine and add some shading to give definition to its overall form.

STEP 6
Now ink over your finished pencil drawing.

STEP 7

To color the Spinosaurus, use a very pale sand color for the base and apply it all over the dinosaur's skin. Next add a lime green tone on top of the base. Finish off by using a grass green over the top. Add tone, shadow, and details using a midrange gray, especially in all the creases. Finally, color the spinal fin with bright fuschia pink and gray and yellow markings.

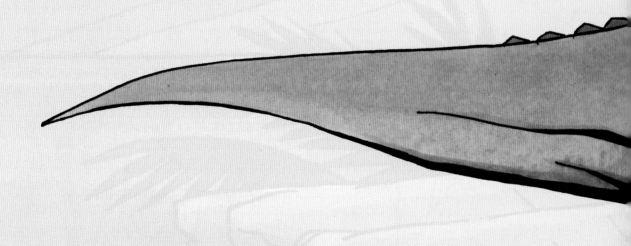

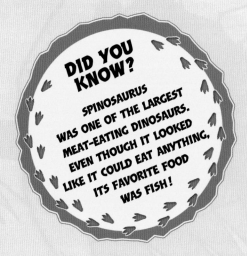

DID YOU KNOW?

SPINOSAURUS WAS ONE OF THE LARGEST MEAT-EATING DINOSAURS. EVEN THOUGH IT LOOKED LIKE IT COULD EAT ANYTHING, ITS FAVORITE FOOD WAS FISH!

ARGENTINOSAURUS

DINO FACT FILE

Argentinosaurus is the largest land animal ever discovered. This plant-eating giant measured 115 feet (35 m) in length and was as tall as a six-story building. Each of its massive backbones was the height of a human. It was so heavy that the ground would have shook as it moved. It's thought that they moved in herds of 20—that must have felt like an earthquake!

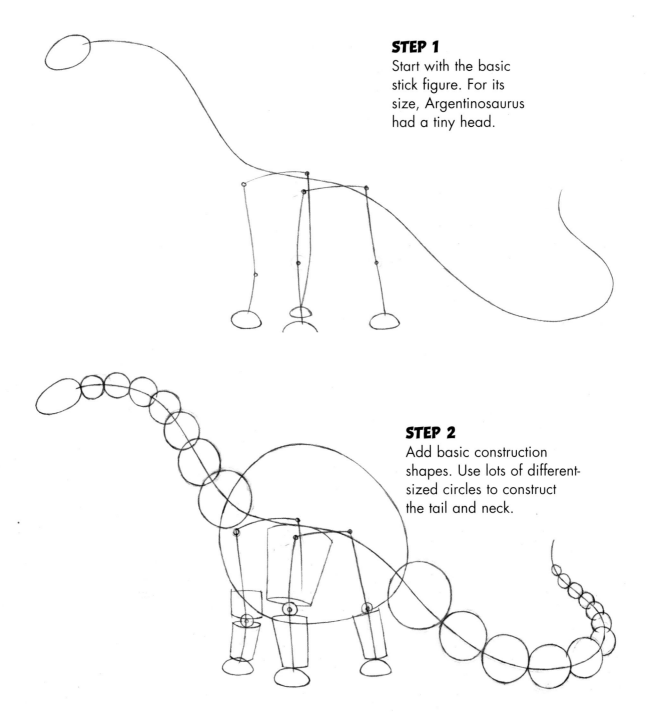

STEP 1

Start with the basic stick figure. For its size, Argentinosaurus had a tiny head.

STEP 2

Add basic construction shapes. Use lots of different-sized circles to construct the tail and neck.

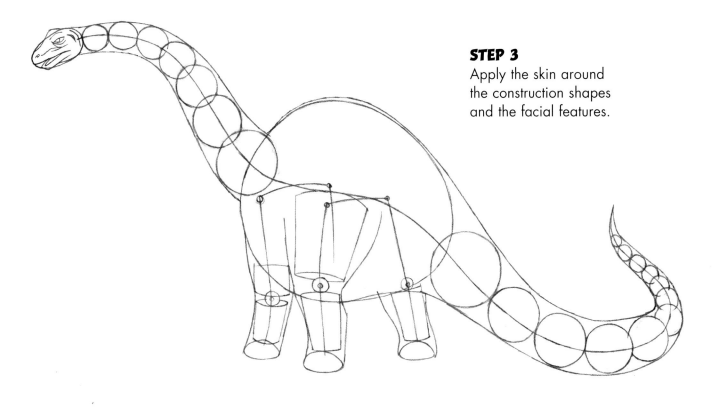

STEP 3
Apply the skin around the construction shapes and the facial features.

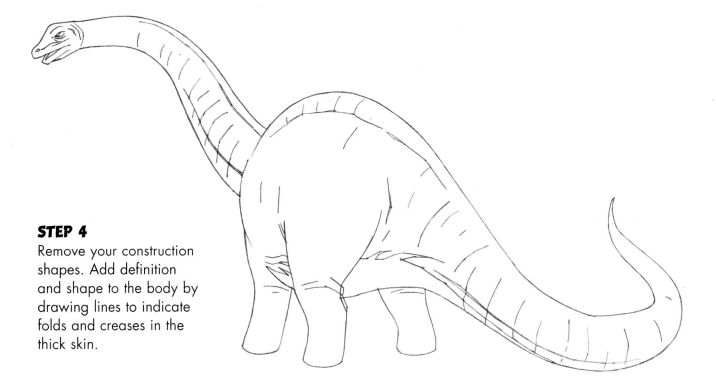

STEP 4
Remove your construction shapes. Add definition and shape to the body by drawing lines to indicate folds and creases in the thick skin.

STEP 5

Complete the final pencil drawing. Finalize all the details on the skin, adding more wrinkles and creases. Then add shading under its belly and on its back leg.

STEP 6

Ink over the pencil
drawing, use a variety
of line thicknesses for
the creases in its skin
for extra depth.

DID YOU KNOW?

ARGENTINOSAURUS NEEDED A LOT OF FOOD TO FUEL ITS HUGE BODY. IT COULD EAT UP TO 100 TONS (91 T) EVERY DAY— THAT'S THE WEIGHT OF A BLUE WHALE!

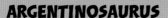

STEP 7

Now it's time to color the Argentinosaurus.
First apply a light gray all over the skin. On top of
the gray base color apply a sand color. Use a very
pale olive green to add shading to the neck and
along the spine. Finish off the dinosaur using a dark
gray to bring out the folds and creases in the skin.

CREATING A SCENE

LANDSCAPE FEATURING GIGANOTOSAURUS

Giganotosaurus lived about 100 million years ago. This was the golden age of dinosaurs, before their mass extinction. Many incredible creatures had evolved and this diversity was also found in the plants, flowers, and landscapes on Earth. Giganotosaurus roamed the plains and valleys of Argentina, South America, where it would hunt giant plant eaters.

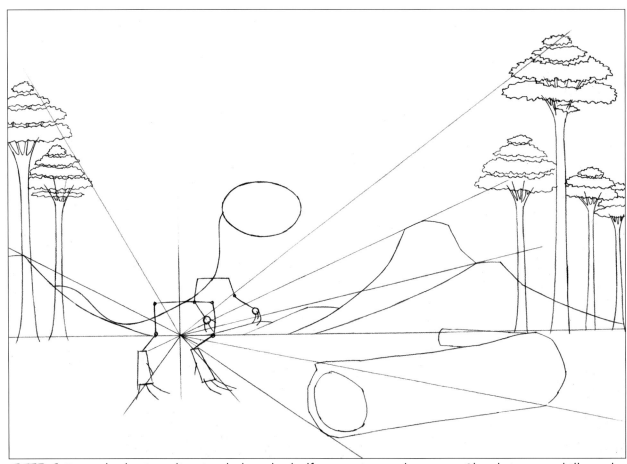

STEP 1 Draw the horizon line just below the halfway point on the page. Sketch in some hills and trees. Draw the stick figure for a Giganotosaurus. Add a fallen tree trunk in the foreground and some leaves on the trees in the background.

STEP 2 Construct the Giganotosaurus (see pages 9–13 for the step-by-step guide). Draw some fernlike plants in the foreground and develop the rock of the mountain.

STEP 3 Draw some smaller bushes in the background and in front of the mountains on the horizon line. Add clouds in the sky. Add skin and teeth to the Giganotosaurus.

STEP 4 Complete the pencil drawing by adding shading to create areas of black and all your final details to the dinosaur and scenery.

STEP 5 Finally, color your prehistoric landscape. You could experiment with other colors to create different effects.

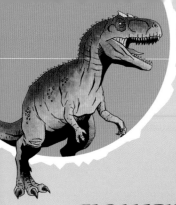

GLOSSARY

cylinders (SIH-len-derz) Shapes with straight sides and circular ends of equal size.

facial (FAY-shul) Of the face.

fierce (FEERS) Strong and ready to fight.

gouache (GWAHSH) A mixture of nontransparent watercolor paint and gum.

mechanical pencil (mih-KA-nih-kul PENT-sul) A pencil with replaceable lead that may be advanced as needed.

sable brushes (SAY-bel BRUSH-ez) Artists' brushes made with the hairs of a sable, a small mammal from northern Asia.

stick figure (STIK FIH-gyur) A simple drawing of a creature with single lines for the head, neck, body, legs, and tail.

structure (STRUK-cher) Form.

tone (TOHN) Any of the possible shades of a particular color.

watercolor (WAH-ter-kuh-ler) Paint made by mixing pigments (substances that give something its color) with water.

INDEX

WEB SITES

Due to the changing nature of Internet links, PowerKids Press has developed an online list of Web sites related to the subject of this book. This site is updated regularly. Please use this link to access the list:
www.powerkidslinks.com/ddino/giganoto/